PRAYERS OF THE COSMOS

PRAYERS OF THE COSMOS

Meditations on the Aramaic Words of Jesus

Translated and with Commentary by
Neil Douglas-Klotz

Foreword by Matthew Fox

HarperSanFrancisco
An Imprint of HarperCollinsPublishers

HarperCollins Web Site: http://www.harpercollins.com

HarperCollins®, 📖 ®, and HarperSanFrancisco™ are trademarks of HarperCollins Publishers, Inc.

FIRST HARPERCOLLINS PAPERBACK EDITION PUBLISHED IN 1994

Library of Congress Cataloging-in-Publication Data

Douglas-Klotz, Neil.
    Prayers of the cosmos: meditations on the Aramaic words of
Jesus / translated and with commentary by Neil Douglas-Klotz;
foreword by Matthew Fox. — 1st ed.
    ISBN 0–06–061994–5
    ISBN 0–06–061995–3 (pbk)
    1. Lord's prayer—Meditations. 2. Beatitudes—Meditations.
3. Jesus Christ—Words—Meditations. 4. Aramaic language—
Translating into English. 5. Bible. N.T. Gospels—Language,
style. I. Bible. N.T. Gospels. English. Selections. 1990.
II. Title.
BV230.D684   1990
226'.9042—dc20   90–30946

01 RRD-H 20 19 18

For Kamae, who teaches me to persevere.
"Blessed are those who plant peace each season."

Contents

Foreword

Reader beware: though this book is brief, it contains the seeds of a revolution.

Those who understand what is at stake in a paradigm shift will immediately grasp the power in this little book. A paradigm shift requires a new pair of glasses by which to look anew at our inherited treasures. Just as all translations of our mystics are affected by the ideology or worldview of the translator, so the same is true of the translations of our Scriptures. Those who have lost a cosmology and the mysticism that accompanies it hardly recognize that fact when they translate the Bible for us.

Yet Scripture, as the monks of old who chanted it daily have attested, must be experienced with the heart and not just studied with the head. So much biblical training in our times tests young scholars for the latter but does little to foster the former. Mysticism—banished from our academic life for three centuries—rarely emerges on the printed page of translators who become steeped in the words but not necessarily the music of the author's spirit and intention. When scriptural passages become overly familiar, matters of rote, memorized prayers instead of living words, religion is paralyzed and loses its capacity for transformation. Scripture then becomes the property of specialists.

How disturbing and refreshing, therefore, is this effort by Neil Douglas-Klotz to recover the original language, the native Middle Eastern language, the Aramaic that Jesus spoke! How much expanded heart consciousness and prophetic juice might result from hearing, for example, that what we have translated as "be you perfect" really means "be you all-embracing," or that "to be satisfied" means "to be surrounded by fruit"; that "blessed are the meek, for they shall inherit the earth" also means "soften what's rigid inside and you shall receive physical vigor and strength from the universe"; that "blessed are the pure in heart" means blessed are those "whose passion is electrified by deep, abiding purpose";

that "heaven" in Aramaic means, in fact, "the universe"; and that the overly familiar words "lead us not into temptation" can be translated in this way: "Don't let surface things delude us, but free us from what holds us back." Can we get any more cosmological than that? Do the words of Jesus not take on new life and vigor in this version of his saying?

Douglas-Klotz's translations also reveal how feminist Jesus was. Consider that the word Jesus uses, which we have traditionally translated as "kingdom," is related to the word for the "Great Mother" in the Middle East; the word we translate as "daily bread" means nourishment of all kinds and derives from roots for the divine feminine and for Holy Wisdom, or Sophia.

Prayers of the Cosmos is not a book *about* mysticism in the Bible. It is a practical meditation that can draw the mystic out of the reader once again, just as the mystic who heard the startling words of Jesus two thousand years ago was drawn out. This is a book that allows us to experience the Scriptures once again through the heart, which means through the body, which means on earth, the source and origin of our bodies. Douglas-Klotz's dedication to bringing the mystic out of self and others through the Dances of Universal Peace is highlighted in the practical and bodily prayer forms that he recommends for recovering the living, breathing Scriptures. He teaches us truly to pray the Scriptures anew, to understand prayer as more than reading or talking. If Hildegard of Bingen was correct eight centuries ago in defining prayer as "breathing in and breathing out the one breath of the universe," then Douglas-Klotz is also correct in insisting that we dance—that is, breathe—the Scriptures anew.

Douglas-Klotz's version of the Lord's Prayer is like a commentary in itself. For centuries theologians have offered us commentaries on this prayer of Jesus, but this one is like no other. It embraces, grounds, challenges. It opens our hearts to cosmology once again—as Jesus was open to cosmology and as all native persons are. It allows the mysticism of our scriptural heritage to move us once again, maybe even to transform us.

I welcome this book and the rich fruit it is sure to bear.

MATTHEW FOX, FOUNDING DIRECTOR
INSTITUTE OF CULTURE AND CREATION SPIRITUALITY

Acknowledgments

In addition to those mentioned in the introduction, my thanks go to many friends, students, teachers, and co-workers who have encouraged me over the years in this project. These include Matthew Fox and the students and faculty of the Institute of Culture and Creation Spirituality in Oakland, California, Murshida Vera J. Corda, Br. Joseph Kilikevice, O.P., Murshid Moineddin Jablonski, Pir Vilayat Inayat Khan, the late Frida Waterhouse, Jodean Johnson, Violetta Reiser, Zamyat Kirby, Tasnim Fernandez, and many others. Special thanks go to the Vedanta Society of San Francisco and the monks of its rural retreat center for providing and preserving the sacred atmosphere of nature in which this work could be completed.

Pronunciation of the Aramaic Words

The transcription of the Aramaic words into English characters is not meant to be a formal, scholarly transliteration. The latter would have required the reader to learn yet another alphabet with special characters, and this book is meant to be used by lay persons. The transcription used is very helpful when used in combination with a pronunciation/chanting cassette tape I have prepared and which is available from various offices of the Dances of Universal Peace network in North America and Europe, as mentioned in the resource list at the end of the book.

PRAYERS OF THE COSMOS

Introduction

The richness of expression present in the native Aramaic language of Jesus is a treasure that has been lost—or limited only to scholars—for too long. To discover this treasure, we must challenge ourselves to participate in the prophetic and mystical tradition that Jesus has represented. It is a far cry from our ordinary way of thinking.

A tradition of both native Middle Eastern and Hebraic mysticism says that each statement of sacred teaching must be examined from at least three points of view: the intellectual, the metaphorical, and the universal (or mystical). From the first viewpoint, we consider the face value of the words in question—what so-called modern people normally call the "literal" meaning. According to native Middle Eastern mysticism, however, each Aramaic word presents several possible "literal" translations. "Blessed are the meek, for they shall inherit the earth" could as easily be translated "Blessed are the gentle" or "Blessed are those who have softened the rigidity within." The word for "earth" in Aramaic also carries the meanings of "earthiness," "the natural abundance of nature," and "everything that appears in particular forms." To understand how all these relate to one another, we must go further.

From the second viewpoint, we consider how a statement or story presents a metaphor for our lives—or the life of a community. Here we must awaken our poetic sensibility: we must participate in re-creating meaning from several possible literal translations. With reference to the above saying of Jesus, where are the rigid places in our lives—or in the life of our society? How do they prevent us from receiving sustenance from the natural abundance of nature?

From the third viewpoint, the universal or mystical, one comes to a truth of the experience pointed to by a particular statement. Here we must go beyond seeing a prayer as an affirmation or petition, or a parable as mere metaphor. We must embrace the wordless experience to which the living words of a mystic point. To continue the above example: one faces the question, What do the words *rigid* and *soft* have to do with my experience of life, of the cosmos, of God? What feelings do the sounds of the key words in Aramaic evoke? How do I act responsibly from this new understanding? There are no set answers to these questions: they challenge us to an individual response.

To a native Middle Eastern mystic like Jesus, none of these viewpoints excludes the others. One holds all the possible meanings of key sacred phrases and prayer and lets them work inside. According to the Hebrew sage and language scholar Fabre D'Olivet (1815) in *The Hebraic Tongue Restored*, the tragedy of biblical translation has been that expressions meant to resonate many levels of meaning—at least the intellectual, metaphorical, and universal—have been whittled down to become "wholly gross in [their] nature . . . restricted to material and particular expressions." This tendency to divide and overliteralize was reflected in the whole Newtonian era: a period that repressed mystical cosmology was also ill at ease with mystical translation. An unnatural division between God, Nature and humanity, unknown to people who lived close to the earth, crept into our language with the advent of modern civilization.

Some of the difficulty harkens back to the source of our texts—and our thinking. Most of the English translations of the words of Jesus come from Greek, a language that differs greatly from Aramaic. Aramaic was the common spoken language throughout the Middle East at the time of Jesus and the tongue in which he expressed his teachings. (Hebrew was primarily a temple language at this time.) According to some scholars, Aramaic was a derivative of ancient Hebrew; others say that Aramaic itself is older, and based on still more ancient Middle Eastern roots. Although Greek was introduced into the Middle East after the conquest of Alexander the Great, it never became the language of the native peoples. Aramaic served as the lingua franca until it was replaced by a derivative tongue, Arabic, during the rise of Islam. Even so, Aramaic continued to be spoken widely in the Middle East into the nineteenth century and is still used in parts of Syria, as well as in the entire church of the East.

Unlike Greek, Aramaic does not draw sharp lines between means and ends, or between an inner quality and an outer action. Both are always present. When Jesus refers to the "kingdom of heaven," this kingdom is always both *within* and *among* us. Likewise, "neighbor" is both inside and outside, as is the "self" that we are to love to the same degree as our "neighbor." Unlike Greek, Aramaic presents a fluid and holistic view of the cosmos. The arbitrary borders found in Greek between "mind," "body," and "spirit" fall away.

Furthermore, like its sister languages Hebrew and Arabic, Aramaic can express many layers of meaning. Words are organized and defined based on a poetic root-and-pattern system, so that each word may have several meanings, at first seemingly unrelated, but upon contemplation revealing an inner connection. The same word may be translated, for instance, as "name," "light," "sound," or "experience." Confronted with such variety, one needs to look at each word or phrase from several different points of view—the ones mentioned above, and possibly others. Jesus showed a mastery of this use of transformative language, which survives even through inadequate translations.

In addition, the Aramaic language is close to the earth, rich in images of planting and harvesting, full of views of the natural wonder of the cosmos. "Heaven" in Aramaic ceases to be a metaphysical concept and presents the image of "light and sound shining through all creation." Like its native Middle Eastern predecessors and like other ancient native languages around the planet, Aramaic is rich in sound-meaning; that is, one can feel direction, color, movement, and other sensations as certain sacred words resonate in the body. This body resonance was another layer of meaning for the hearers of Jesus' words and for the native Middle Eastern mystic. In fact, this writer finds similarities between some of the most important words used by Jesus and words used in native Middle Eastern chants for thousands of years before his time.

Organization of This Book

Because of these special qualities of Aramaic and of Jewish mysticism, I was challenged to devise a structure that would begin to reveal the many facets shining in each statement, much as one would view the various facets of a cut crystal. The majority of this volume considers the lines of the Lord's Prayer in Aramaic. This cleansing prayer helps us remember what is important in life and contains the central themes in Jesus' sayings. These themes portray a cycle of renewal revealing a spiral journey through stages like those presented by the "four paths" of creation spirituality: the paths of original blessing, letting go, breakthrough, and compassion.

First, each line of the prayer is rendered according to the root meaning of the words, but from several different points of view, as indicated above. Second, textual notes are given so that the reader may begin to understand the richness of the Aramaic roots and make his or her own connections or alternate translations (the metaphorical level). Third, I have added open-ended meditations or "body prayers," which point toward an experience of the words of Jesus in one's body and life. These body prayers encourage one to participate in the *sound and feeling* of the words as well as their intellectual or metaphorical meaning. To come close to the experience that Jesus offered his hearers, we must extend our understanding beyond what we call the "mind" to the whole self. This is the mystical or universal level of interpretation.

The basis of these body meditations stems from work passed on orally in the native Middle Eastern mystical tradition for thousands of years. I have modified and reworked these for use by people today. There are no longer any "secrets" that are not already in plain view for those who can understand them. I feel that the need of the earth is so great that we must do everything helpful to reestablish harmony with all creation.

Following the Lord's Prayer, I have included versions of the Beatitudes—a rich source of Jesus' teaching but often confusing to the reader in present translation. These and the other sayings from the Gospels that follow show that including the mystical level of translation clears up a number of difficulties. I have also provided for comparison parallel renderings for each section from the King James Version. In most cases (where there is not outright mistranslation), these versions are not wrong, but so limited in expression that they have proved misleading. I do not believe that any of the more modern versions are substantially better; in each case where the Greek text has been taken as a source, translations have spawned theological concepts that are foreign to Aramaic thinking as well as, I believe, the thinking of Jesus himself.

Texts Used

My source for the Aramaic text is a version of the Syriac Aramaic manuscript of the Gospels, also known as the Peshitta Version, that was prepared by the Reverend G. H. Gwilliam and issued by the Clarendon Press in 1901. This version is available through the United Bible Societies. There is yet considerable scholarly controversy concerning the age and authority of the Peshitta and other early biblical manuscripts.

Some biblical scholars believe that at least the Gospel of Matthew was first written in Aramaic and the other Gospels drawn either from this text or from another hypothetical Aramaic document known as "Q" (from German *Quelle,* "source"). Other scholars regard Mark as the earliest Gospel, largely because it is the shortest and was, perhaps, a "shorthand" version. Still other (primarily Eastern) scholars maintain that all of the Gospels were originally written in Aramaic, since they were all intended for either Jewish or Gentile (but still Aramaic-speaking) listeners. For further information, the reader may refer to the resource list at the end of this book.

As Dr. George M. Lamsa, the pioneering Aramaic scholar of the 1930s, has pointed out in his *Holy Bible from Ancient Eastern Manuscripts,* the church of the East regards the Peshitta as the oldest and most authoritative version of the Bible. Peshitta means "simple," "sincere," or "true." With regard to the words of Jesus, this version may be as old as the second century A.D., according to some Eastern Christian scholars.

The church of the East holds that if the Peshitta does not contain the oldest version, it is still much closer to the thought forms of Jesus than any Greek version. As Lamsa points out in his *New Testament Origin,* there is much internal evidence to prove this. Most of the idiomatic confusions in the parables of Jesus are instantly cleared up when looked at from the Aramaic point of view. These confusions arose when translators worked from Latin versions of Greek versions that themselves misunderstood the Aramaic.

In all the religions of humankind, the sacred teachings have always been written down in the language of the founder. There is no question that Jesus and his followers spoke Aramaic. In addition, all the early Christian churches were Semitic in origin. The gospel was written first for the Jews and the "lost sheep of the house of Israel," who were also Aramaic speakers.

According to Lamsa in *New Testament Origin,* "Not a word of either the Old or the New Testament was originally written in Greek or any other European language. The theory that Jesus' teaching was first recorded in Greek was undoubtedly prompted by anti-Semitism. . . . Prior to the British occupation of India and Egypt, the Western world knew hardly anything about the East. Almost everything which was written in Germany, England and America relative to Eastern Christianity was conjectural or biased. Therefore the whole body of evidence relative to the Bible theology and the people of the East must be re-examined in the light of the present findings and the Aramaic language" (pp. 1, 17–18).

Further, the prejudice toward Greek versions of the Gospels as "most authoritative" recapitulates the general ignorance of and prejudice against native peoples and their cultures on the part of "civilized man" for hundreds of years. Fortunately, this is beginning to change. Most Western schools, however, still teach that "real culture began with the Greeks," a fact largely discredited by the archaeological and anthropological findings of recent decades. What we value in classical Greek art, music, and spirituality, according to Riane Eisler in *The Chalice and the Blade,* seems to have been largely taken over from previous cultures that worshiped the Great Mother and attained a high degree of culture in a partnership society largely free of war and conflict.

Native peoples in the Middle East also had a rich language, culture, and spirituality for thousands of years before Jesus. His inspired use of many older sacred phrases, reaching back even beyond the Hebrew tradition, shows that a native mystical tradition did survive, probably in hiding or in the desert, both before and throughout the rise of orthodox Judaism, Christianity, and Islam. Some schools of Sufism claim to be among the inheritors of this native Middle Eastern tradition, which precedes even the Egyptian mystery schools.

Those interested in further researches in the Aramaic language are referred to the works of Dr. George M. Lamsa and those of his student and scholarly heir, Dr. Rocco A. Errico. In particular, I am indebted to Dr. Errico for his warm help and referral to Aramaic language resources as well as the published Peshitta edition he has used in his studies. Dr. Errico is currently working on a new Aramaic grammar that will make learning the basics of the language much easier than it is with the texts now available (see the resources list at the end of this book).

My own research in Middle Eastern languages, which began fourteen years ago, has proceeded from an interest in the original meanings and sound-values of sacred words from the Semitic language traditions. My inspiration was Samuel L. Lewis, a scholar and mystic schooled in Kaballah (Jewish mysticism) as well as Christianity, Sufism, Buddhism, and Hinduism. My innovation beyond the work of Drs. Lamsa and Errico has been into the realm of the mystical expression of Jesus, the third level, particularly as it is found in the Aramaic roots of his words.

As a native Assyrian, Lamsa was primarily interested in the idiomatic level, and his own translation of the Bible corrects hundreds of mistakes of this type that occur in other texts (see reference list). To approach the third level of translation, one must not only acquire language skills but also study the science of sound and letters common to the Middle Eastern mystical traditions. This science points to states of meditation and awareness that must be experienced, not just studied intellectually. In this work, therefore, I have approached Jesus' words as a translator, poet, student, and teacher of native mysticism, rather than as a theologian. These translations are my own, and the reader is free to call them versions or commentaries if this helps to assimilate them. The effect of the "mystical" is not to mystify, but to return us to a better relationship with the cosmos, which is the heritage of all native traditions.

As my main source for deeper interpretation of Aramaic roots, I have used Fabre D'Olivet's *The Hebraic Tongue Restored*. Although written in 1815, this is still a primary published reference for the complete interpretation of these roots; the material survives elsewhere as an oral tradition in Jewish mysticism (Kaballah) and Sufism. D'Olivet includes many cross-references to other Middle Eastern languages. Because there is as yet no complete Aramaic-English dictionary, one must search for additional help in various Syriac lexicons and keys to the Peshitta. In addition to the study of Aramaic, I have also drawn from my language research into Arabic, a tongue that evolved from Aramaic.

All the major contemporary traditions of the Middle East—Jewish, Christian, and Islamic—stem from the same source, the same earth, and probably the same language. All originally called God either *El* or *Al*, which means "That," "the One," or "that One which expresses itself uniquely through all things." From this root arises the sacred names *Elat* (Old Canaanite), *Elohim* (Hebrew), *Allaha* (Aramaic), and *Allah* (Arabic). If this simple fact became better known, I believe there would be much more tolerance and understanding among those who consciously or unconsciously perpetuate prejudice between what are essentially brother-sister traditions.

The poetic form of most of my English versions is the "long line" used in the verse of Walt Whitman and William Blake. In this regard, I am indebted to the suggestion of American poet Robert Bly, who pointed out this form's sonorous, rolling qualities, similar to the tones of the King James version of the Bible. In addition, I have included an approximate transliteration of the Aramaic characters into English so that readers may sound out the original and feel its tempo, rhythm, and vibration as part of their own body prayer. Allowing for the fact that several dialects of Aramaic exist and that this book is intended for nonscholars, I have sacrificed some accuracy in the transliteration in order to use regular English characters rather than linguistic symbols. Interested scholars may refer to the reference list at the end of this book for resources on learning to read the Aramaic characters or for recordings of them being read and sung.

Questions may arise about this work simply because I have approached the words of Jesus rather than those of another mystic. "Are these versions literal?" "Are they inspired, like the Authorized Version?" These questions presume a certain theological orientation, based largely on beliefs with which I do not wish to quarrel. As I have indicated, there may be many "literal" versions of the same passage in Aramaic. Regarding the second question, I believe that inspiration is as available today as it was in the time of King James—and available in the living experience of those who have followed in the footsteps of Jesus. Jesus was neither a scholar nor a theologian; his words ring across the ages, even in limited translation, and strike at the heart of our dilemmas and questions. From this work, I hope and pray that many "inspired translations" may occur—in both the transformed words and the actions of those who confront the Cosmic Christ through the words of the Aramaic Jesus.

NEIL DOUGLAS-KLOTZ

—THE LORD'S PRAYER—

The Lord's Prayer (Aramaic)

ܐܒܘܢ ܕܒܫܡܝܐ ܢܬܩܕܫ ܫܡܟ ✴ ܬܐܬܐ ܡܠܟܘܬܟ ܂ ܢܗܘܐ
ܨܒܝܢܟ ܂ ܐܝܟܢܐ ܕܒܫܡܝܐ ܂ ܐܦ ܒܐܪܥܐ ✴ ܗܒ ܠܢ ܠܚܡܐ ܕܣܘܢܩܢܢ
ܝܘܡܢܐ ✴ ܘܫܒܘܩ ܠܢ ܚܘܒܝܢ ܂ ܐܝܟܢܐ ܕܐܦ ܚܢܢ ܫܒܩܢ ܠܚܝܒܝܢ ✴ ܘܠܐ
ܬܥܠܢ ܠܢܣܝܘܢܐ ܂ ܐܠܐ ܦܨܢ ܡܢ ܒܝܫܐ ܂ ܡܛܠ ܕܕܝܠܟ ܗܝ ܡܠܟܘܬܐ
ܘܚܝܠܐ ܘܬܫܒܘܚܬܐ ܠܥܠܡ ܥܠܡܝܢ ܂ ܐܡܝܢ ܂

Abwoon d'bwashmaya

Nethqadash shmakh

Teytey malkuthakh

Nehwey tzevyanach aykanna d'bwashmaya aph b'arha.

Hawvlan lachma d'sunqanan yaomana.

Washboqlan khaubayn (wakhtahayn)
    aykana daph khnan shbwoqan l'khayyabayn.

Wela tahlan l'nesyuna

Ela patzan min bisha.

Metol dilakhie malkutha wahayla wateshbukhta l'ahlam
almin.

Ameyn.

The Lord's Prayer (King James English Translation)

Our Father which art in heaven

Hallowed be thy name.

Thy kingdom come.

Thy will be done in earth, as it is in heaven.

Give us this day our daily bread.

And forgive us our debts, as we forgive our debtors.

And lead us not into temptation, but deliver us from evil.

For thine is the kingdom, and the power, and the glory, for ever.

Amen.

(Matthew 6:9–13, King James Version)

1. Our Birth in Unity

Abwoon d'bwashmaya ܐܰܒܘܢ ܕܒܫܡܝܐ

(KJV version: *Our Father which art in heaven*)

O Birther! Father-Mother of the Cosmos,
you create all that moves
in light.

O Thou! The Breathing Life of all,
Creator of the Shimmering Sound that
touches us.

Respiration of all worlds,
we hear you breathing—in and out—
in silence.

Source of Sound: in the roar and the whisper,
in the breeze and the whirlwind, we
hear your Name.

Radiant One: You shine within us,
outside us—even darkness shines—when
we remember.

Name of names, our small identity
unravels in you, you give it back
as a lesson.

Wordless Action, Silent Potency—
where ears and eyes awaken, there
heaven comes.

O Birther! Father-Mother of the Cosmos!

Textual Notes

The prayer begins with an expression of the divine creation and the blessing that emanates from all parenting. The ancient Middle Eastern root *ab* refers to all fruit, all germination proceeding from the source of Unity. This root came to be used in the Aramaic word for personal father—*abba*—but still echoes its original ungendered root in sound-meaning. While *abwoon* is a derivative of this word for personal father, its original roots do not specify a gender and could be translated "divine parent." These roots reveal many levels of meaning. *Bwn* shows the ray or emanation of that father/motherhood proceeding from potential to actual, here and now. In Aramaic, the character for *b* may also be pronounced *w* or include shades of both. An Aramaic scholar, the Reverend Mar Aprem (1981), notes that the same root (*ab*) may stand for personal father or spiritual father, depending on whether the *w* (for personal) or the *b* (for spiritual) is emphasized. No doubt, Jesus meant there to be an echo of both, as Aramaic is rich in this sublime wordplay.

Further, according to the mystical science of sounds and letters, common to both Aramaic and Hebrew, the word *abwoon* points beyond our changing concepts of "male" and "female" to a cosmic birthing process. At this level of interpretation, *abwoon* may be said to have four parts to its sound-meaning:

A: the Absolute, the Only Being, the pure Oneness and Unity, source of all power and stability (echoing to the ancient sacred sound *AL* and the Aramaic word for God, *Alaha*, literally, "the Oneness").

bw: a birthing, a creation, a flow of blessing, as if from the "interior" of this Oneness to us.

oo: the breath or spirit that carries this flow, echoing the sound of breathing and including all forces we now call magnetism, wind, electricity, and more. This sound is linked to the Aramaic phrase *rukha d'qoodsha*, which was later translated as "Holy Spirit."

n: the vibration of this creative breath from Oneness as it touches and interpenetrates form. There must be a substance that this force touches, moves, and changes. This sound echoes the earth, and the body here vibrates as we intone the whole name slowly: *Ah-bw-oo-n.*

The rest of the phrase completes the motion of divine creation. In *d'bwashmaya,* the central root is found in the middle: *shm.* From this root comes the word *shem,* which may mean light, sound, vibration, name, or word. The root *shm* indicates that which "rises and shines in space," the entire sphere of a being. In this sense, one's name included one's sound, vibration, or atmosphere, and names were carefully given and received. Here the "sign" or "name" that renders *Abwoon* knowable is the entire universe. The ending *-aya* shows that this shining includes every center of activity, every place we see, as well as the potential abilities of all things. In effect, *shmaya* says that the vibration or word by which one can recognize the Oneness—God's name—*is* the universe. This was the Aramaic conception of "heaven." This word is central to many of the sayings of Jesus and usually misunderstood. In Greek and later in English, "heaven" became a metaphysical concept out of touch with the processes of creation. It is difficult for the Western mind to comprehend how one word can have such seemingly different meanings. Yet this was the worldview of the native Middle Eastern mystic.

Body Prayers

In the first line of Jesus' prayer, we remember our origins—not in guilt or imperfection, but in blessing and unity, in both vibration and stillness. For the divine breath (*rukha*) touches even the absence of what we can measure as "light" or "sound."

1. Intone the sound *Ah-bw-oo-n* slowly, finding a pitch that resonates the most in your body. Take some time to find this "note"—it is your own heritage from *Abwoon:* the tone at which you vibrate most is part of your "name," in the Aramaic meaning of the word. Feel the vibration of the sound. Where do you feel it in your body? As the sound enters the silence, let yourself follow it there. Begin to feel all the movements within the body—heartbeat, breathing, peristalsis—that go on without our attention. Feel these movements as internal prayers that point to the gift and responsibility of co-creation with God.

2. When in nature, walking or sitting, breathe in feeling the sound *Abwoon* inside yourself, and breathe out feeling the sound *d'bwashmaya.* Feel breath come into you as it does into the grass, trees, rocks, and water. Feel the One Source of this breathing. And feel the breathing returning to all creation. Our breath feeds the plants and theirs us. The exchange unites us in God. All creation says the holy Name silently.

3. When at work, breathe in feeling the sound *Ah;* breathe out feeling the sound *bwoon.* As you inhale, feel all newness and nourishment coming into the heart-lungs area. As you exhale, feel everything old, everything that wants to be released, leaving with the breath. Where in the body can you feel the breath? What parts are not aware and could use waking up? As we become aware of the body, the darkness, the inside, we begin to be aware of soul (Aramaic, *naphsha*) and on the track of the kingdom/queendom within.

2. Clearing Space for the Name to Live

Nethqadash shmakh   ܢܶܬܩܰܕܰܫ ܫܡܳܟ.

(KJV version: *Hallowed be thy name*)

> Focus your light within us—make it useful:
> as the rays of a beacon
> show the way.
>
> Help us breathe one holy breath
> feeling only you—this creates a shrine
> inside, in wholeness.
>
> Help us let go, clear the space inside
> of busy forgetfulness: so the
> Name comes to live.
>
> Your name, your sound can move us
> if we tune our hearts as instruments
> for its tone.
>
> Hear the one Sound that created all others,
> in this way the Name is hallowed
> in silence.
>
> In peace the Name resides:
> a "room of one's own," a holy of holies
> open, giving light, to all.
>
> We all look elsewhere for this light—
> it draws us out of ourselves—but the Name
> always lives within.
>
> Focus your light within us—make it useful!

Textual Notes

In the second line of the prayer, the root *shm*—the divine name, light, sound, experience—returns in a more specific form. In the first line, *shem* was spread throughout the universe; it was part of the underlying Unity in which everything lives. Here we affirm that the name will become *qadash*, "holy" (from which the Hebrew word *kāshēr*, "kosher," is drawn). In Aramaic, one makes a thing holy by setting it apart, separating it for a specific purpose. Because this Aramaic construct occurs equally inside as well as outside of us, we might say that when we separate something, hold it inviolate, we create for it a holy place within.

The roots of *nethqadash* also evoke the images of clearing or sweeping and of preparing the ground for an important plant. In one of the most beautiful pictures presented by the Aramaic, the roots show a person bending his or her head over a special place where seeds are sown, indicating also that one bends over the heart and plants devotion and perseverance at the same time.

The inner shrine by which God's name is hallowed can be developed only through letting go, releasing some of the clutter inside that keeps us too busy to be silent and receptive to the "still, small voice." The prayer also leads us to consider our "feeling heart," the place that mystics of all paths have called the inner temple. Jesus recommended going to this "heart-shrine" (one of the meanings of "enter into thy closet"—Matt. 6:6) whenever we pray. In another setting, Virginia Woolf called this "a room of one's own." When this inner shrine is established, it becomes possible to be, in the words of Jesus, "all-embracing" (usually translated as "perfect") even as our Creator-source is all-embracing (Matt. 5:48).

In Aramaic, the prayer always directs us in a practical fashion. To make the experience of *Abwoon* useful, we need to create a place for this Oneness to live inside. Then the light of *shem*—the clarity or intelligence that arises in ultimate peace—becomes usable on an everyday basis, like light in a lamp.

Body Prayers

To create this holy place inside, some letting go is necessary. If the room is filled with old knickknacks, there is no space for a shrine. If the flute is clogged, no music can come through. The sounds of this phrase indicate a way to begin this letting go: they lead us to a sensation of the heart-lungs area. Here blood and air collaborate to let go of what's needed with each exhalation, to take in what's needed with each inhalation. In our daily routine, we can let go and set aside time for silence, meditation, and prayer. Even while engaged in work, we can breathe one conscious breath, letting go into God's creative light and Name.

1. Create a separate place in your home, your room, your life where you can let go and breathe, feeling that as you breathe, God does also. Sit or lie in a relaxed position and notice the rising and falling of the breath. Breathe in feeling the sound *nethqadash* (nith-qah-dahsh) and breathe out feeling the sound *shmakh* (shm-ah-kh). Simply relax and breathe, feeling more and more letting go inside, creating space for the breath of God. Notice the beating of the heart and the rhythm of the breath as it goes in and out. Can they begin to create a music together, a pattern? Let this feeling of the breathing and heartbeat working together begin to create a place of silence and peace inside. Underneath this peace is an energized fullness—all action is possible. The silence is the shrine, the room. The fullness is the Name, God's light.

2. Anytime while engaged in work or action, take one long deep breath remembering this holy of holies within. The Name can become hallowed again, in an instant. Or: feel the sound of the phrase *nethqadash shmakh* inside. Let any small movements that this sound creates clear a space and bring you back to peace.

3. At another time, relax and feel the shrine created by the heartbeat and breathing. Notice which parts of the body feel enlivened by the meditation. Then notice those parts that feel separate or absent. Do not judge any as good or bad. Simple notice and accept them with unconditional love.

3. The Creative Fire

Teytey malkuthakh ܬܐܬܐ ܡܠܟܘܬܟ

(KJV version: *Thy kingdom come*)

Create your reign of unity now—
through our fiery hearts
and willing hands.

Let your counsel rule our lives,
clearing our intention
for co-creation.

Unite our "I can" to yours, so that
we walk as kings and queens
with every creature.

Desire with and through us
the rule of universal fruitfulness
onto the earth.

Your rule springs into existence
as our arms reach out to
embrace all creation.

Come into the bedroom of our hearts,
prepare us for the marriage of
power and beauty.

From this divine union, let us birth
new images for a new world
of peace.

Create your reign of unity now!

Textual Notes

In the third line of the prayer, the holy space inside is used as a workshop to envision and prepare for new creation. *Teytey* means "come" but includes the images of mutual desire, definition of a goal, and, in the old sense, a "nuptial chamber"—a place where mutual desire is fulfilled and birthing begins.

Malkuthakh refers to a quality of rulership and ruling principles that guide our lives toward unity. It could justifiably be translated as either "kingdom" or "queendom." From the ancient roots, the word carries the image of a "fruitful arm" poised to create, or a coiled spring that is ready to unwind with all the verdant potential of the earth. It is what says "I can" within us and is willing, despite all odds, to take a step in a new direction.

The word *Malkatuh*, based on the same root, was a name of the Great Mother in the Middle East thousands of years before Jesus. The ancients saw in the earth and all around them a divine quality that everywhere takes responsibility and says "I can." Later those who expressed this quality clearly were recognized as natural leaders—what we call queens or kings.

In a collective sense, *malkuthakh* can also refer to the counsel by which anything is ruled, the collective ideals of a nation, or the planet. In this line, we ask that the kingdom/queendom come by clarifying our personal and collective ideas in alignment with the Creator's—toward unity and creativity like the earth's.

Body Prayers

Once we have created an interior temple of peace and devotion, this heart-place can be used to clarify our goals and to break through to a new sense of creativity in our lives. With the help of the One, we discover a new sense of "I can." The birth of this creative power happens in childhood when one begins to feel (and say), "I can do it *myself!*" In meditation on this line of the prayer, one begins to discover that the small "I" can unite with the larger and only *I*, what Jesus called *Alaha*, the Oneness or God.

1. While lying or sitting, return to the peaceful place inside created by feeling your heartbeat and breathing. As the medieval mystic Hildegard of Bingen said, everything may be felt a "feather on the breath of God." Listen to music that inspires you and notice its effect on your inner shrine. Do any images arise? At another time, you might focus on inspirational art, on a creative solution to a problem that confronts you, or on clear guidance for your next step. Or you might rhythmically breathe a short prayer or any line of the Lord's Prayer (for instance, breathing in *teytey*, breathing out *malkuthakh*). Let the meditation on and in the heart keep you close to the heartbeat of God.

2. While walking, breathe and move together in rhythm. Feel yourself as if drawn from the heart toward a goal or person you love. Try actually moving *from the heart* and notice the effect. At first, make sure you have enough room to move without being interrupted. With some practice, this body prayer can also be used "in the crowd" to help fortify one's feeling and refocus one's intention.

3. When in need of healing or rest, or in emotional turmoil, return to the heart-shrine. Let whatever feelings emerge be embraced and acknowledged by the breath of God in your own breathing. Gradually allow the breathing to become more rhythmic. Inhale from the One Source of healing; exhale to that part of yourself in need or turmoil.

4. Heaven Comes to Earth: Universal Compassion

Nehwey tzevyanach aykanna d'bwashmaya aph b'arha

ܢܗܘܐ ܨܒܝܢܟ݈ܝ: ܐܝܟܢܐ ܕܒܫܡܝܐ: ܐܦ ܒܐܪܥܐ.

(KJV version: *Thy will be done in earth, as it is in heaven*)

Your one desire then acts with ours,
as in all light, so in
all forms.

Let all wills move together
in your vortex, as stars and planets
swirl through the sky.

Help us love beyond our ideals
and sprout acts of compassion
for all creatures.

As we find your love in ours,
let heaven and nature form
a new creation.

Unite the crowd within
in a vision of passionate purpose:
light mates with form.

Create in me a divine cooperation—
from many selves, one voice,
one action.

Let your heart's fervent desire
unite heaven and earth
through our harmony.

Your one desire then acts with ours,
as in all light, so in
all forms.

Textual Notes

In this fourth and most central line of the prayer, heaven meets earth in acts of compassion. We have remembered our source in *Abwoon*, the source of all parenting. We have let go to clear a holy place inside for this realization to live. From this new beginning we have clarified our goals, realized the power of our co-creation, and envisioned our next step. Now we are ready to act. In one sense, Jesus presented a prayer for all humanity, one that all creation joins in each moment. In another sense, he presented a very practical method by which to approach any undertaking or to renew one's purpose in life.

Tzevyanach can be translated as "will," but it is not what we usually think of as willpower (trying hard) or willfulness (unrestrained force). In Aramaic, the word carries the meaning of "desire," a harmonious cooperation of movement that includes natural discipline. This kind of "heart's desire" means that one's goal or purpose has moved beyond the mental or ideal stage. It has become so much a part of oneself that one need no longer think about it. One's whole being moves toward the goal with certainty. The ancient roots of the word summon forth images of a vortex of harmony and generation, of a host of stars swirling through the heavens.

Aykanna ("just as") carries the sense of a determined desire toward consistency and stability. We pray that God's heart-desire be done consistently through our lives in form as it is in sound (word) and light (image or vision).

Arha means "earth"; in fact, it may be the original source of that word. In sound-meaning it evokes the sigh of the human species whenever it feels the support of the earth underneath and remembers to treat it as another living being, rather than an object to be exploited. Behind that, the old Hebrew roots carry the meaning of all nature, all natural gatherings of mass and form produced by the universal force *AR*—power with movement. From this root, we also get our word *ardor*.

Body Prayers

At this stage, the prayer exhorts us to proceed beyond getting ready for creation, beyond our ideas and creative imagination, to take responsibility for our actions and the way they affect our surroundings. This rules out creativity that does not take the community and the well-being of the earth into consideration. We must act and take the consequences. We may reach the goal we have envisioned, or we may "fail." The prayer, however, points us to a universe where every winter is followed by a spring, and God acts in and with the cycle of creation. When we have focused our action by beginning with remembrance of *Abwoon*, we will have carried out our part; we can plant and then leave the fruits to the Creator.

1. Upon finding yourself caught in a habitual response—to relationships, work, or any other life situation—that does not further your purpose, use the body prayer of the inner shrine to clear space and envision a new response. Sometimes the action envisioned in a prayerful state will not make sense. Breathe *Abwoon* and ask God for confirmation. The action will never go against your conscience. Envision it so clearly that you feel it in your body. Then when the situation arises, act from the heart, before the mind can drag you back to a habitual response.

2. Make a list of what you feel is lacking in life, both personally and globally. Then make another list of what inspires you, again including your personal qualities and strengths as well as those you feel around you on the earth. Compare the feeling that you had making each list and hold the two feelings together in your heart. While holding both, see what relation you find between what's wanting and what's fulfilled in your life (as well as the life of the planet). What are the most important areas for change? Then with lists in hand, compare these areas to the way you spend most of your time. Use a peaceful, prayerful breath and do not be sidetracked by either guilt or self-satisfaction. Use this process as a plan for your practical short-term as well as long-term goals. Find one immediate action that will make a difference, no matter how small.

3. Lying down for a few minutes in comfortable surroundings, return to the shrine of the inner heart. Meditate on the feeling of your bones as they are supported from underneath by the earth.

Feel supported for your own weight—no more, no less. Visualize and feel the bone marrow, the deepest part of yourself from which a vital part of the immune system comes. Cells from the bone marrow are responsible for creating antibodies to merge with whatever enters the body and is seen as "not yourself." Other immune cells from the thymus gland, near the heart, percolate through the body and communicate what is needed for each moment. Visualize the denseness of bone, the expansiveness of heart, and feel the body's natural capacity to change *not-self* into *self*—to merge with the "enemy" and make it part of unity, part of the whole. For a few minutes join with these deep pulsations of the body as a prayer for unity in the world.

Consider the prevalence of immune-system diseases in our society today. What are we being asked to learn about "differences" and "enemies"?

5. The Blessings of Earthiness: The Next Step

Hawvlan lachma d'sunqanan yaomana

هَبْ لَمْ لَكْسَمَا دِسْهِمِتَنْ نَهُمَنَا.

(KJV version: *Give us this day our daily bread*)

Grant what we need each day in bread and insight:
subsistence for the call of
growing life.

Give us the food we need to grow
through each new day,
through each illumination of life's needs.

Let the measure of our need be earthiness:
give all things simple, verdant,
passionate.

Produce in us, for us, the possible:
each only-human step toward home
lit up.

Help us fulfill what lies within
the circle of our lives: each day we ask
no more, no less.

Animate the earth within us: we then
feel the Wisdom underneath
supporting all.

Generate through us the bread of life:
we hold only what is asked to feed
the next mouth.

Grant what we need each day in bread and insight.

Textual Notes

A word very rich in meaning, *lachma* is both "bread" and "understanding"—food for all forms of growth and for elementary life in general. It is derived from a more basic root relating to the divine feminine—*HMA*—which pictures growing vigor, verdancy, warmth, passion, possibility, and all instruments of this generative power. This root became the word *hochma*, translated as "Holy Wisdom" in Proverbs. As we saw earlier, the *h* and *oo* sounds point toward the breath, this time the breath that returns to and emanates from the earth with the eternal cry of the mother,—*ma*. Later this root would be rendered by the Greek word *Sophia*, referring to an embodiment of all feminine wisdom.

Sunqanan refers to needs, but may also mean "an illumined measure," "a circle of possession," or "a nest." *Hawvlan* can mean "give," "humanly generate," "produce with life and soul," or "animate with fruit." This part of the prayer reminds us in many ways that sometimes what we need is not only the grand picture of unity and God's creation, but also the "next step"—just food or understanding for this moment.

In the first half of the prayer we remember the One and feel our blessing from the cosmos. In the second half we begin a new cycle of blessing, but in an even more embodied and practical way: we face each other and remember the divine Many. This section begins from the earth up. The prayer pushes us beyond an introverted spirituality to consider everything in our dealings with others. In reminding us of "understanding," the prayer points to what always stands under and supports us—the Mother Earth. We can make that support more real by feeding each other. We can also treasure the source of that bread by not hoarding or demanding from the earth more than we need, by respecting the source of our most basic support.

Body Prayers

As human beings, one of the most precious things we can give one another is our complete understanding and support, each day and each moment as we are able, with all our perceived limitations included. As we make this simple here-and-now contact with one another, we share the real embodiment. Perhaps this is part of what Jesus meant when, in breaking bread the night before he died, he said, "This is my body." He may also have been directing his disciples back to simple, human concerns: the need to feed someone who is hungry, to visit someone who is sick or in prison.

1. While lying down, come to a feeling of support through all the bones: let your attention roam naturally from point to point where you feel the earth supporting you underneath. Does one shoulder feel more in contact than the other? Or one hip more than the other? By making these small comparisons, begin to experience how you relate to the earth on a bodily level. Then slowly stand up and walk meditatively, step by step, feeling the earth's support through all your bones. Body researchers have found that very little (or no) muscle action may be necessary to walk. One could simply let gravity and the felt support of ligaments and bones do the work by leaning slightly forward and "being walked."

As you walk, experience how much you hold yourself away from the earth or press down upon it. Feel the support of the earth for whatever you naturally offer it, for whoever you are, for your right to be here without the necessity of constant busyness. This is an excellent meditation for working with a body sense of blessing and self-esteem. You may also broaden your meditation to consider the way we walk upon the earth as a species: the earth holds a memory of our treatment of it. When we neither oppress it or ask it to carry more than our own weight nor hold ourselves away in a detached and introverted pietism, we will begin to right the balance as a planet. As Jesus said, "Feed my lambs . . . feed my sheep" (John 21:15–16).

2. This body prayer is best done with a partner. Let one person lie down and experience his or her own sense of support through Mother Earth. Sitting near this person's feet, let the partner also feel support through the bones and then share this sense of sup-

port by gradually and gently lifting one of the partner's legs. Let the contact be simple, without expectations or demands—simply sharing support felt through the earth for a minute or two. The reclining partner may notice any sensations or feelings as more letting go occurs.

After the partner's touch has ended, the one lying down may feel any differences in sensation between the two sides of the body. Continue the meditation by shifting to contact through the other side as well. Then let the reclining partner slowly stand at his or her own pace, as if standing for the first time, and experience any change in support. The active and receptive partners may then switch and afterward share what they experienced through this mutual meditation on *lachma*, the bread of understanding and life.

3. Intone the sound *lachma* (lah-ch-mah) slowly, feeling how the phrase becomes denser inside. There is more to work through and we are reminded to take things "step by step," not forcing beyond the needs of the time. What do we need for *this moment* of our lives?

6. Letting Go, Heartbeat by Heartbeat

Washboqlan khaubayn (wakhtahayn) aykanna daph khnan shbwoqan l'khayyabayn

ܘܫܒܘܩܠܢ ܚܘܒܝܢ: ܘܚܛܗܝܢ ܕܝܟ ܣܢ ܚܢܢ ܠܝܣܒܬܝ .
ܘܫܒܘܩܢ ܠܢ ܣܟܠܘܬܢ:

(KJV version: *And forgive us our debts, as we forgive our debtors*)

Loose the cords of mistakes binding us,
as we release the strands we hold
of others' guilt.

Forgive our hidden past, the secret shames,
as we consistently forgive
what others hide.

Lighten our load of secret debts as
we relieve others of their
need to repay.

Erase the inner marks our failures make,
just as we scrub our hearts
of others' faults.

Absorb our frustrated hopes and dreams,
as we embrace those of others
with emptiness.

Untangle the knots within
so that we can mend our hearts'
simple ties to others.

Compost our inner, stolen fruit
as we forgive others the spoils of
their trespassing.

Loose the cords of mistakes binding us,
as we release the strands we hold
of others' guilt.

Textual Notes

Just as the previous line invokes a more embodied, earthy sense of blessing, so this line asks for a deeper letting go: forgiveness. This is another gift that we can give one another, an opportunity to let go of the mistakes that tie ourselves and one another in knots. The "trespassing" that we release is not only against one another, but also against the earth and all creatures.

Besides "forgive," the roots of the first word (wa)*shboqlan* may also be translated "return to its original state," "reciprocally absorb," "reestablish slender ties to," and "embrace with emptiness." The prayer reaffirms that our original state is clear and unburdened, one where our slender ties to creation are based on mutual releasing, with every breath we breathe.

In Matthew's version of the prayer, the word *khaubayn* was translated as "debts" or "offenses" from the Greek. Its alternative meanings are "hidden past," "secret debt," "hidden, stolen property," and any "inner fruit" that affects the intelligence and the soul negatively. In the version of the prayer in Luke, the word *khtahayn* is used and usually translated as "sins." From the Aramaic, it could also be rendered as "failures," "mistakes," "accidental offenses," "frustrated hopes," or "tangled threads"—the latter implying that some mending or restoration is needed. I have chosen to include both words in these versions, since they are very similar in sound. It is as likely that Jesus said both as that he said one but not the other. The word *aykanna* ("just as") again reminds us (as in line four) that releasing must be done consistently and regularly if our knotted relationships are to become whole and stable again.

Body Prayers

The sounds of this line return us to the feeling of heart and blood—washing, flowing, asking that we release anything unwanted in the same way that our blood carries refuse from every part of the body to the lungs to be released with each breath.

1. Lie comfortably and feel the heartbeat and pulsing of the blood, this time focusing on its releasing power. If you have difficulty feeling your blood pulse, try placing one hand lightly cupped near the heart. Rather than *reach* for the pulse, imagine your hand *listening* to it, receptively. Feel and visualize the blood bringing to the lungs everything that wants to be released this moment. This is breathed out. With each new breath, new life is brought in and pulses back out to every cell of the body. As the pulsing quality of this "body forgiveness" is felt, the muscles also relax to allow the veins, arteries, and capillaries more space and easier flow. Past tensions being held in the muscles may begin to release; old habits and "armor" that we sometimes confuse with our natural selves begin to let go. Perhaps this is part of what Jesus meant when, in offering a cup of wine the night before the crucifixion, he said, "This is my blood, given for the untying of mistakes and failures."

2. The above prayer may also be done in pairs, with one person lying down and the other holding the feet (as in the previous line). In this case, the intention is that both are releasing into the cosmos and that the person sitting helps the partner by adding to his or her awareness of heartbeat. Both connect their body awareness on the level of the heartbeat and blood; the person lying down is receptive and allows his or her pulsation to be supported by the person sitting. In a group, the same thing may be done with all joining hands in a circle, standing or sitting, meditating in unity with the group pulse. As we contact the deeper layers of ourselves, the slower rhythms of awareness, we find an embodied source of meditation. Forgiveness is here, *now*—not outside somewhere.

3. Try intoning the words of this line of the prayer: they take patience.* The many *kh* sounds continue to bring us back to places

---

* (Wa-shbōq-láhn khow-báyn wa-kh-tah-hāyn eye-káhna daph kh-nan sh-bó-qan l'kh-eye-ya-bāyn.)

in the body where we need to release. The sounds themselves seem to say that we must recognize and acknowledge our knots, including offenses against ourselves, before they can be untied. (There are actually four levels of *h* sound in Aramaic—soft, medium, hard, and very hard. Mystically, each level indicates the primordial life force coming more and more into manifestation. The *h* sound used in the above words are the second level—the misdirected life has not become completely hardened; there is yet a chance for renewal.)

7. Remembrance: The Birth of New Creation and Liberty

Wela tahlan l'nesyuna
Ela patzan min bisha

ܘܠܐ ܬܥܠܢ ܠܢܣܝܘܢܐ܃
ܐܠܐ ܦܨܢ ܡܢ ܒܝܫܐ܂

(KJV version: *And lead us not into temptation, but deliver us from evil*)

Don't let surface things delude us,
But free us from what holds us back
(from our true purpose).

Don't let us enter forgetfulness,
the temptation of false
appearances.

(To the fraud of inner vacillation—
like a flag tossed in the wind—
alert us.)

But break the hold of unripeness,
the inner stagnation that
prevents good fruit.

(From the evil of injustice—
the green fruit and the rotten—
grant us liberty.)

Deceived neither by the outer
nor the inner—free us to
walk your path with joy.

Keep us from hoarding false wealth,
and from the inner shame of
help not given in time.

Don't let surface things delude us,
But free us from what holds us back.

Textual Notes

These are probably the least understood and, because of the Greek version, the most mistranslated lines in the prayer. In the Aramaic version, no one outside "leads us into temptation"—least of all God. *Wela tahlan* could be translated "don't let us enter," "don't let us be seduced by the appearance of," or "don't let us heap up what's false or illusory in." *Nesyuna* could be translated as "temptation," in the Aramaic sense of something that leads to inner vacillation or agitation, diverting us from the purpose of our lives. The old roots call up the picture of a flag waving in the wind—blown here and there—like a mind rendered uncertain by the seductions of materialism (including spiritual materialism). It is the picture of forgetfulness: a losing of oneself in appearances, a failure to look deeper when the situation calls for it.

Having involved ourselves in the work of justice (bread) and compassion (forgiveness) in the preceding lines, we come again to see our limitations as well as all the pain and suffering that we cause ourselves and the rest of creation. The prayer here reminds us not to forget our origins in creation and the divine Breath, nor to "burn out" over all that needs to be done. This line goes together with the next to push us toward a new breakthrough into joy.

Ela patzan min bisha was translated "but deliver us from evil." *Bisha* does mean "evil" or "error" but in the Hebraic and Aramaic sense of "unripeness" or inappropriate action. The roots point toward a sense of what delays or diverts us from advancing, as well as a sense of inner shame for not producing good fruit—the right action at the right time. *Patzan* could also be translated "loosen the hold of," "give liberty from," or "break the seal that binds us to."

This line finishes the statement of the previous one: don't let us be deluded by the surface of life, but neither let us become so inward and self-absorbed that we cannot act simply and humanly *at the right time.* The prayer reminds us that sometimes our ideals—including those of holiness, peace, and unity—carry us into the future or the past and make it difficult to be in the present where help is needed now.

Body Prayers

The sounds of these last two lines allow one's breathing to become more refined again after the denseness of the line on forgiveness. The prayer does not say there will never be forgetfulness (temptation) or unripeness (evil). It does not deny limitation, nor the unripe acts against humanity and nature that are our responsibility to correct. But it reminds us to take them in the light of God's whole picture. We can release all our limiting concepts, including those about the prayer we have been meditating upon. We can release our concepts of both unity and separateness. In the end, these too are just doors, fingers pointing toward the unspeakable and mysterious Reality.

1. Find a place that allows you to walk unhindered and unencumbered—either in nature or freely indoors in a circle. As you walk, with each step become more present just to your own footfalls, *now.* Walk simply being present. Wherever you find a part of yourself that resists, be present with and accept that part also. Continue to include and embrace whatever thoughts and feelings come up. As you walk, feel yourself fully and completely accepted in the presence of God.

2. Buddhists present the tradition of Maitreya Buddha, the *bodhisattva* or messenger who has agreed to forego personal salvation and enlightenment until all other beings have attained them. Something like the picture of Maitreya Buddha is presented by these two lines of the prayer. That part of ourselves that feels as though it will be the last to wake up to the presence of the divine also serves a purpose in God's universe. Forgetfulness and unripeness may be the keys to our own perfection and draw us together as a planet, as we realize how fragile life can be. A walking meditation from the Buddhist tradition asks us to take time to walk as though we were stepping on the heads of all beings—not gingerly or holding ourselves away from the earth but with compassion and openheartedness.

8. A Celebration of Cosmic Renewal

Metol dilakhie malkutha wahayla wateshbukhta l'ahlam almin.
Ameyn.

ܡܛܠ ܕܕܝܠܟ ܗܝ ܡܠܟܘܬܐ ܡܢܐ ܡܥܬܣܬܐ ܠܥܠܡ ܥܠܡܝܢ ܐܡܝܢ .

(KJV version: *For thine is the kingdom, and the power, and the glory, for ever. Amen.*)

From you is born all ruling will,
the power and life to do, the song that beautifies all—
from age to age it renews.

To you belongs each fertile function:
ideals, energy, glorious harmony—
during every cosmic cycle.

Out of you, the queen- and kingship—
ruling principles, the "I can"
of the cosmos . . .

Out of you, the vital force
producing and sustaining all life,
every virtue . . .

Out of you the astonishing fire,
the birthing glory, returning light and sound
to the cosmos . . .

Again and again, from each universal gathering—
of creatures, nations, planets, time, and space—
to the next.

Truly—power to these statements—
may they be the ground from which all
my actions grow:
Sealed in trust and faith.

Amen.

Textual Notes

Scholars do not agree on whether this line was originally contained in the prayer of Jesus. Much of the discussion revolves around how old and authoritative one judges the Aramaic Peshitta version of Matthew to be (see Introduction). Matthew's version contains the line; Luke's does not. The author tends to side with a compromise approach—that of Joachim Jeremias (1964). Jeremias contends that if this closing did not occur, one very similar to it would have been used, in keeping with the closing of other Jewish prayers. In addition, in the Aramaic this closing perfectly summarizes the main themes of the prayer and recapitulates the spiral journey that it presents.

At the end, we return to the creative visioning of God, the power to accomplish these visions, and the beauty that adds grace and artistry to them. The old roots of *dilakhie* present more than the idea of simple possession ("For thine is the kingdom . . ."); they show another planting image: a field fertile and abundant, one sufficient to produce everything. *Malkutha* reprises the theme of the cosmic "I can," the royalty that permeates the universe. *Hayla* refers to the life force or energy that produces and sustains. In this sense, it is not "power over" but power in unison with all natural creation. *Teshbukhta* may be translated as "glory" but calls forth more exactly the image of a "song"—a glorious harmony returning divine light and sound to matter in equilibrium. The roots of the word also present the picture of a "generative fire that leads to astonishment."

L'ahlam almin is an Aramaic idiom meaning "from age to age"; "for ever and ever" is much too abstract. The Aramaic roots literally mean "from gathering to gathering." The ancient Middle Eastern view of life pictured the entire cosmos—force, physical reality, planets, nature, human beings—slowly gathering and assembling to a central point, then slowly dispersing again. This cycle of gathering defined the ancient sense of time or "ages." This perspective parallels certain discoveries of the New Physics and provides an antidote for our modern, rushed sense of "time out of joint."

The word *ameyn* sealed agreements in the Middle East: it was a solemn oath (and probably better than our written contracts). Behind this word, which could also be translated "truly," was the sense of giving "power to" whatever form or words preceded it. It has continued to carry this sense in the tradition of gospel music. From its older roots, *ameyn* presents the image of the ground from which a particular future growth will occur. One can trace the same sound-meaning back to the ancient Egyptian sacred word *Ament*, which pointed to the mysterious ground of being or underworld holding the secrets of life, death, and rebirth. The sound of the word as it is intoned reminds one of the ringing of the bell at the end of a Zen meditation. Somehow, all of oneself comes together once more, instantly, in the moment. The healing—or making whole—is always here and now.

Body Prayers

1. With a gentle breath in and out, feel inside the various steps along the journey that the prayer has presented. Without focusing on its concepts, embrace whatever emotional feelings or body sensations the prayer has evoked and gather them into the inner temple of the heart. Some of these feelings may be pleasant, some unpleasant. Gather them all in and feel them as whole and complete in God's universe as they disperse again to their source.

2. Close your eyes and hear inside the sound of the word *ameyn*. Feel the ground of the earth sprouting the ground of your being as your whole self comes together to go forward with life. Breathe in feeling *ameyn* and breathe out feeling *ameyn*, considering your next step—for the day or your life. Say *"Ameyn!"* and open your eyes.

The Lord's Prayer (One Possible New Translation from the Aramaic)

O Birther! Father-Mother of the Cosmos,

Focus your light within us—make it useful:

Create your reign of unity now—

Your one desire then acts with ours,
as in all light, so in all forms.

Grant what we need each day in bread and insight.

Loose the cords of mistakes binding us,
as we release the strands we hold
of others' guilt.

Don't let surface things delude us,

But free us from what holds us back.

From you is born all ruling will,
the power and the life to do,
the song that beautifies all,
from age to age it renews.

Truly—power to these statements—
may they be the ground from which all
my actions grow: Amen.

—THE BEATITUDES—

The Beatitudes (Aramaic)

ܛܘܼܒܝܗܘܿܢ ܠܡܣܟܹܢܹܐ ܒܪܘܼܚ: ܕܕܝܼܠܗܘܿܢ ܗ̱ܝ ܡܲܠܟܘܼܬܵܐ ܕܲܫܡܲܝܵܐ܂

ܛܘܼܒܝܗܘܿܢ ܠܐܲܒܝܼܠܹܐ ܕܗܹܢܘܿܢ ܢܸܬܒܲܝܐܘܿܢ܂

ܛܘܼܒܝܗܘܿܢ ܠܡܲܟܝܼܟܹ̈ܐ: ܕܗܹܢܘܿܢ ܢܹܐܪܬܘܿܢ ܠܐܲܪܥܵܐ܂

ܛܘܼܒܝܗܘܿܢ ܠܐܲܝܠܹܝܢ ܕܟܲܦܢܝܼܢ ܘܲܨܗܹܝܢ ܠܟܹܐܢܘܼܬܵܐ: ܕܗܹܢܘܿܢ ܢܸܣܒܥܘܿܢ܂

ܛܘܼܒܝܗܘܿܢ ܠܲܡܪܲܚ̈ܡܵܢܹܐ: ܕܲܥܠܲܝܗܘܿܢ ܢܸܗܘܘܿܢ ܪ̈ܲܚܡܹܐ܂

ܛܘܼܒܝܗܘܿܢ ܠܐܲܝܠܹܝܢ ܕܲܕܟܹܝܢ ܒܠܸܒܗܘܿܢ: ܕܗܹܢܘܿܢ ܢܸܚܙܘܿܢ ܠܐܲܠܵܗܵܐ܂

ܛܘܼܒܝܗܘܿܢ ܠܥܵܒ̈ܕܲܝ ܫܠܵܡܵܐ: ܕܲܒܢܲܘ̈ܗܝ ܕܐܲܠܵܗܵܐ ܢܸܬܩܪܘܿܢ܂

ܛܘܼܒܝܗܘܿܢ ܠܐܲܝܠܹܝܢ ܕܐܸܬܪܕܸܦܘ ܡܸܛܠ ܟܹܐܢܘܼܬܵܐ: ܕܕܝܼܠܗܘܿܢ ܗ̱ܝ ܡܲܠܟܘܼܬܵܐ ܕܲܫܡܲܝܵܐ܂

ܛܘܼܒܲܝܟܘܿܢ ܐܸܡܲܬܝ ܕܲܡܚܲܣܕܝܼܢ ܠܟܘܿܢ ܘܪܵܕܦܝܼܢ ܠܟܘܿܢ: ܘܐܵܡܪܝܼܢ ܥܠܲܝܟܘܿܢ ܟܠ ܡܸܠܵܐ ܒܝܼܫܵܐ ܡܸܛܠܵܬܝ ܒܕܲܓܵܠܘܼܬܵܐ܂ ✴ ܗܵܝܕܹܝܢ ܚܕܵܘ ܘܲܪܘܲܙܘ: ܕܐܲܓܪܟܘܿܢ ܣܓܝܼ ܒܲܫܡܲܝܵܐ܂ ܗܵܟܲܢܵܐ ܓܹܝܪ ܪܕܲܦܘ ܠܲܢܒ̈ܝܹܐ ܕܡܸܢ ܩܕܵܡܲܝܟܘܿܢ܂

Tubwayhun l'meskenaee b'rukh d'dilhounhie malkutha
dashmaya.
Tubwayhun lawile d'hinnon netbayun.
Tubwayhun l'makikhe d'hinnon nertun arha.
Tubwayhun layleyn d'kaphneen watzheyn l'khenuta
d'hinnon nisbhun.
Tubwayhun lamrahmane dalayhun nehwun rahme.
Tubwayhun layleyn dadkeyn b'lebhon d'hinnon nehzun
l'alaha.
Tubwayhun lahwvday shlama dawnaw(hie) d'alaha nitqarun.
Tubwayhun layleyn detrdep metol khenuta dilhon(hie)
malkutha dashmaya.
Tubwayhun immath damhasdeen l'khon waradpin l'khon
wamrin elaykon kul milla bisha metolath b'dagalutha.

Haydeyn khadaw wa rwazw dagarkhun sgee bashmaya
hakana geyr r'dapw l'nabiya d'men q'damaykun.

The Beatitudes (King James English Translation)

Blessed are the poor in spirit: for theirs is the kingdom of heaven.
Blessed are they that mourn: for they shall be comforted.
Blessed are the meek: for they shall inherit the earth.
Blessed are they which do hunger and thirst after righteousness: for they shall be filled.
Blessed are the merciful: for they shall obtain mercy.
Blessed are the pure in heart: for they shall see God.
Blessed are the peacemakers: for they shall be called the children of God.
Blessed are they which are persecuted for righteousness' sake: for theirs is the kingdom of heaven.
Blessed are ye, when men shall revile you, and persecute you, and shall say all manner of evil against you falsely, for my sake.

Rejoice, and be exceedingly glad: for great is your reward in heaven: for so persecuted they the prophets which were before you.

(Matthew 5:3–12, King James Version)

Jesus said:

Tubwayhun l'meskenaee b'rukh d'dilhounhie malkutha d'ashmaya.

ܛܘܒܝܗܘܢ ܠܡܣܟܢܐ ܒܪܘܚ ܿ ܕܕܝܠܗܘܢ ܗܝ ܡܠܟܘܬܐ ܕܫܡܝܐ.

(KJV version: *Blessed are the poor in spirit: for theirs is the kingdom of heaven.*)

Happy and aligned with the One are those who find their home in the breathing; to them belong the inner kingdom and queendom of heaven.

Blessed are those who are refined in breath; they shall find their ruling principles and ideals guided by God's light.

Tuned to the Source are those who live by breathing Unity; their "I can!" is included in God's.

Healthy are those who devotedly hold fast to the spirit of life; holding them is the cosmic Ruler of all that shines and rises.

Resisting corruption, possessing integrity are those whose breath forms a luminous sphere; they hear the universal Word and feel the earth's power to accomplish it through their own hands.

Healed are those who devote themselves to the link of spirit; the design of the universe is rendered through their form.

Textual Notes

The first of the Beatitudes was translated as "Blessed are the poor in spirit: for theirs is the kingdom of heaven." The Aramaic word *meskenaee* encompasses the images of a solid home base or resting point, of a fluid, round, luminous enclosure, and of devotedly holding fast to something—as if one were "poor" for lack of it. The word *rukh* may be translated as "spirit," "breath," "soul" or as whatever moves, stirs, animates, and links us to life.

The Greek translators appear to have been at a total loss with these seemingly different meanings united around the image of the entire universe filled with one cosmic breath of life, the *rukha d'qoodsha* or Holy Breath. "Poor in spirit" is a traditional Aramaic idiom meaning "humble," according to Dr. George Lamsa (1936). Behind this, the roots tell us that when one is attuned through the breath to God, one does not put oneself forward inappropriately. One's readiness for action rests in the eternal silence of God's Name.

As we saw in the Lord's Prayer, *malkutha* is a word that Jesus used often. It is the "I can"—the queendom and kingdom of the universe, from the personal through the cosmic. In this case, the "I can" extends through all realms of light, vibration, and name; *dashmaya* is another grammatical form of *d'bashmaya*, found in the first line of the Lord's Prayer.

Body Prayer

When feeling out of rhythm with yourself or your surroundings, experiment with breathing in and out, feeling the sound of the word *rukha* or *Alaha*. Let the rhythm of the word and the rhythm of the breath merge in a way that feels natural. Allow the sensation of the breathing to touch the entire body. Gradually let go of the word and allow the feeling of your breathing to cradle and rock whatever part of yourself has been ignored or starved from its connection with the source of life.

Jesus said:

Tubwayhun lawile d'hinnon netbayun.

ܛܘܒܝܗܘܢ ܠܐܒܝܠܐ ܕܗܢܘܢ ܢܬܒܝܐܘܢ .

(KJV version: *Blessed are they that mourn: for they shall be comforted.*)

Blessed are those in emotional turmoil; they shall be united inside by love.

Healthy are those weak and overextended for their purpose; they shall feel their inner flow of strength return.

Healed are those who weep for their frustrated desire; they shall see the face of fulfillment in a new form.

Aligned with the One are the mourners; they shall be comforted.

Tuned to the Source are those feeling deeply confused by life; they shall be returned from their wandering.

Textual Notes

This second Beatitude was translated, "Blessed are they that mourn: for they shall be comforted." *Lawile* can mean "mourners" (as translated from the Greek), but in Aramaic it also carries the sense of those who long deeply for something to occur, those troubled or in emotional turmoil, or those who are weak and in want from such longing. *Netbayun* can mean "comforted," but also connotes being returned from wandering, united inside by love, feeling an inner continuity, or seeing the arrival of (literally, the face of) what one longs for.

Body Prayer

When in emotional turmoil—or unable to feel clearly any emotion—experiment in this fashion: breathe in while feeling the word *lawile* (lah-wee-ley); breathe out while feeling the word *net-bayun* (net-bah-yoon). Embrace all of what you feel and allow all emotions to wash through as though you were standing under a gentle waterfall. Follow this flow back to its source and find there the spring from which all emotion arises. At this source, consider what emotion has meaning for the moment, what action or nonaction is important *now.*

Jesus said:

Tubwayhun l'makikhe d'hinnon nertun arha.

ܠܘܿܒܼܘܿܗܝ ܠܡܟܼܝܟܼܐ : ܕܗܢܘܿܢ ܢܕܼܟܼܗܝ ܐܪܚܐ .

(KJV version: *Blessed are the meek: for they shall inherit the earth.*)

Blessed are the gentle; they shall inherit the earth.

Healthy are those who have softened what is rigid within; they shall receive physical vigor and strength from the universe.

Aligned with the One are the humble, those submitted to God's will; they shall be gifted with the productivity of the earth.

Healed are those who have wept inwardly with the pain of repressed desire; they shall be renewed in sympathy with nature.

Integrated, resisting corruption are those who have dissolved heavy morality within; they shall be open to receive the splendor of earth's fruits.

Textual Notes

This third Beatitude was translated, "Blessed are the meek: for they shall inherit the earth." *L'makikhe* could be translated as "the meek" (as was done from the Greek), but the Aramaic would say "gentle" or "humble." Behind these words, the old roots carry the meaning of one who has softened that which is unnaturally hard within, who has submitted or surrendered to God, or who has liquefied rigidities, heaviness (especially moral heaviness), and the interior pain of repressed desires.

Nertun can mean "inherit," but in the broad sense of receiving from the universal source of strength (*AR*) and reciprocity (*T*). In this case, softening the rigid places within leaves us more open to the real source of power—God acting through all of nature, all earthiness.

Body Prayer

When feeling weak from the busyness of life, take a moment to breath in feeling *makikhe* (mah-kee-key) and breathe out feeling *arha* (ar-ha). Feel what has become tight beginning to loosen. Try visualizing a favorite place in nature that allows you to open up and receive from the bounty of creation. Better yet, go there.

Jesus said:

Tubwayhun layleyn d'kaphneen watzheyn l'khenuta d'hinnon nisbhun.

ܛܘܒܝܗܘܢ ܠܐܝܠܝܢ ܕܟܦܢܝܢ ܘܨܗܝܢ ܠܟܐܢܘܬܐ ܂ ܕܗܢܘܢ ܢܣܒܥܘܢ ܂

(KJV version: *Blessed are they which do hunger and thirst after righteousness: for they shall be filled.*)

Blessed are those who hunger and thirst for physical justice—righteousness; they shall be surrounded by what is needed to sustain their bodies.

Healthy are those who turn their mouths to receive a new birth of universal stability; they shall be encircled by the birth of a new society.

Aligned with the One are those who wait up at night, weakened and dried out inside by the unnatural state of the world; they shall receive satisfaction.

Healed are those who persistently feel inside: "If only I could find new strength and a clear purpose on which to base my life"; they shall be embraced by birthing power.

Integrated, resisting delusion are those who long clearly for a foundation of peace between the warring parts of themselves; they shall find all around them the materials to build it.

Textual Notes

This Beatitude was translated, "Blessed are they which do hunger and thirst after righteousness: for they shall be filled." *Khenuta* was translated as "righteousness," a vague metaphysical term in English. In Aramaic, this word refers to both an inner and an outer sense of justice, a base upon which things can rest, the perfection of natural stability. This includes a sense of physical, inner rightness among the different voices we sometimes feel within, as well as the reflection of these voices in society.

The oldest roots of the Aramaic word *layleyn* ("to those") go back to an image of one watching by night, waiting by lamplight for something to happen. According to the word's ancient roots, this kind of desire creates a vortex of possibility that draws in the object of the heart. Here the ancient sound-meaning of a word generated what we call grammar—in this case, a construction that shows possession and direction toward a person.

The word translated as "hunger" (*d'kaphneen*; literally, "the hungering") may also mean "to turn the mouth toward something," or to long for strengthening the physical being. "Thirst" (*tzheyn*) also conveys an image of being parched inwardly, dried out (we might say "burnt out"). When we long for and finally receive a sense of inner justice and a reestablishment of harmony, we see the purpose of the hunger and thirst. It has created an inner sense of radiance and clarity: the letting go will have been for a purpose. Another planting image from the Aramaic occurs in *nisbhun*, "satisfied," which also means to be "surrounded by fruit," "encircled by birthing," and "embraced by generation."

Body Prayer

For finding a direction: experiment with breathing in and out *khenuta* (khe-noo-tah) or intone the word slowly on one note. Feel the resonance of the final sound *-tah* opening from the heart. If you are making a decision in your life, bring the feeling of the various choices inside to merge with the sensation of the breathing and heartbeat. Which alternative feels that it opens from the heart like the end of the sound? Continue to breathe the sound and try walking with each alternative. Compare the sensation in the body for each alternative. Or, if you are investigating a general direction (not a choice), what images arise from the breathing, sound, and walking in the moment that you come to stillness?

Jesus said:

Tubwayhun lamrahmane dalayhun nehwun rahme.

ܛܘܒܝܗܘܢ ܠܡܪܚܡܢܐ ܆ ܕܥܠܝܗܘܢ ܢܗܘܘܢ ܪܚܡܐ܂

(KJV version: *Blessed are the merciful: for they shall obtain mercy.*)

Blessed are those who, from their inner wombs, birth mercy; they shall feel its warm arms embrace them.

Aligned with the One are the compassionate; upon them shall be compassion.

Healthy are those who extend grace; they shall find their own prayers answered.

Healed are those who extend a long heartfelt breath wherever needed; they shall feel the heat of cosmic ardor.

Tuned to the Source are those who shine from the deepest place in their bodies. Upon them shall be the rays of universal Love.

Textual Notes

This Beatitude was translated, "Blessed are the merciful: for they shall obtain mercy." The key words *lamrahmane* and *rahme* both come from a root later translated as "mercy" from the Greek. The ancient root meant "womb" or an inner motion extending from the center or depths of the body and radiating heat and ardor. The root may also mean "pity," "love," "compassion," a "long drawn breath extending grace," or an "answer to prayer." The association of womb and compassion leads to the image of "birthing mercy." As Meister Eckhart later wrote, "We are all meant to be Mothers of God."

Body Prayer

Slowly intone the root *rahm* (rah-hm), opening to allow the sound to penetrate to the bones and muscles at the base of the pelvis. How could I feel more of my love and compassion this deeply? How could I feel my own birthing struggle connecting with the birthing cries of the earth and all its beings?

Jesus said:

Tubwayhun layleyn dadkeyn b'lebhon d'hinnon nehzun l'alaha.

ܛܘܒܝܗܘܢ ܠܐܝܠܝܢ ܕܕܟܝܢ ܒܠܒܗܘܢ ܀ ܕܗܢܘܢ ܚܠܬܚܙܘܢ ܠܐܠܗܐ ܀

Blessed are the consistent in heart; they shall contemplate the One.

Healthy are those whose passion is electrified by deep, abiding purpose; they shall regard the power that moves and shows itself in all things.

Aligned with the One are those whose lives radiate from a core of love; they shall see God everywhere.

Healed are those who have the courage and audacity to feel abundant inside; they shall envision the furthest extent of life's wealth.

Resisting corruption are those whose natural reaction is sympathy and friendship; they shall be illuminated by a flash of lightning: the Source of the soul's movement in all creatures.

Textual Notes

This Beatitude was translated, "Blessed are the pure in heart: for they shall see God." *Dadkeyn* refers to those "consistent" in love or sympathy, those who have both a natural sense of influence and abundance and a fixed, electrifying purpose. The old roots call up the image of a flower blossoming because that is its nature.

The word translated as heart (*lebhon*) also carries the sense of any center from which life radiates—a sense of expansion plus generative power: vitality, desire, affection, courage, and audacity all rolled into one. *Nehzun* could be translated "see," but also points to inner vision or contemplation. The old roots evoke the image of a flash of lightning that appears suddenly in the sky: insight comes like that. Besides "God" and "the One," the roots of the word *alaha* point to the force and passionate movement of the cosmos through the soul of every living thing. Another image from the roots of *alaha* is the furthest extent of a cosmic force that also possesses identity and can be identified everywhere as: here! this!

Body Prayer

For developing a sense of confidence and "heart": intone *lebhon* (le-bh-oh-n) slowly on one note; visualize and feel the sound coming into the center of the chest and resonating from there (especially on the *n* sound) throughout the body. Continue this, adding the image/feeling of a relationship or project that you would like to be consistent with or see through to the end. See and feel it coming to fruition while intoning *nehzun l'alaha* (neh-zoon l'al-ah-ha).

Jesus said:

Tubwayhun lahwvday shlama dawnaw(hie) d'alaha nitqarun.

ܠܘܒܬܘܦܝ ܠܬܒܕܬܢ ܥܠܟܢ: ܕܝܒܢܬܗܣ ܕܢܠܟܗܢ ܝܐܡܕܦܢ.

(KJV version: *Blessed are the peacemakers: for they shall be called the children of God.*)

Blessed are those who plant peace each season; they shall be named the children of God.

Healthy are those who strike the note that unites; they shall be remembered as rays of the One Unity.

Aligned with the One are those who prepare the ground for all tranquil gatherings; they shall become fountains of Livingness.

Integrated are those who joyfully knit themselves together within; they shall be stamped with the seal of Cosmic Identity.

Healed are those who bear the fruit of sympathy and safety for all; they shall hasten the coming of God's new creation.

Textual Notes

This line was translated, "Blessed are the peacemakers: for they shall be called the children of God." *Lahwvday* refers to those who not only make or perform an action but also are committed to it. The old roots call up more images of planting: tilling the ground, laboring regularly, bringing forth fruit, and celebrating. The emphasis is on that which is done periodically and regularly—despite the odds, as one might say.

The word for "peace" (*shlama*) is essentially the same as that used throughout the Middle East for thousands of years as a greeting. It also means health, safety, a mutual agreement that saves a difficult situation, any happy assembly, or a stroke that unites all parties in sympathy.

The word for "children" (*dawnawhie*) refers to any embodiment, emanation, or active production from that which was only potential before. The roots of the word translated as "shall be called" (*nitqarun*) also present the beautiful image of digging a channel or well that allows water to flow. In this sense, as we "plant peace" we become channels or fountains for hastening the fulfillment of the divine will.

Body Prayer

For peace: breathe in the sound of the word *shlama* (shlah-mah); breathe out the sound *shlama*. What one regular action would make your own life more peaceful? How could this feeling be extended to an action that would include the peacefulness of your community?

Jesus said:

Tubwayhun layleyn detrdep metol khenuta dilhon(hie) malkutha dashmaya.

لحوّجۇچخ خۇنبكم جيخّذ۟ڕ۞ه ميخك جنۇمۂ : جەپخۇچخ ۋنب مُنخمۂ
. جۇمۇۂ

(KJV version: *Blessed are they which are persecuted for righteousness' sake: for theirs is the kingdom of heaven.*)

Blessings to those who are dislocated for the cause of justice; their new home is the province of the universe.

Health to those who are dominated and driven apart because they long for a firm foundation; their domain is created by the Word above, the earth beneath.

Aligned with the One are those who draw shame for their pursuit of natural stability; theirs is the ruling principle of the cosmos.

Healing to those who have been shattered within from seeking perfect rest; holding them to life is heaven's "I can!"

Tuned to the Source are those persecuted for trying to right society's balance; to them belongs the coming king- and queendom.

Textual Notes

This Beatitude was translated "Blessed are they which are persecuted for righteousness' sake: for theirs is the kingdom of heaven." Besides "persecuted," the word *detrdep* can also mean driven, dominated, dislocated, disunited, or moved by scandal or shame. *Khenuta*—that base of inner justice and stability—is the same word referred to in the fourth Beatitude. The recurrence of the phrase *malkutha dashmaya* reminds us of the royalty and power of the universe, as well as its potential: the *shem* or light is in evidence everywhere—don't be afraid to look beyond the boundaries of what you call "home."

In this and the next Beatitude, Jesus presents a realistic picture of what his hearers probably already knew: society does not easily tolerate the prophetic spirit and one is likely to run into opposition. Jesus does not, however, either commiserate with us or incite us to seek suffering. He places the reactiveness of society within a cosmic context: if you are dislocated for justice, consider your new home to be the planet—or the universe. The boundaries that provide our margin of safety sometimes also insulate us from our next step. "Consider adversity as an incitement to take another step" seems to be both the message and the body prayer of these final Beatitudes.

Jesus said:

*Tubwayhun immath damhasdeen l'khon waradpin l'khon wamrin
eleykon kul milla bisha metolath b'dagalutha.*

ܛܘܒܝܟܘܢ ܐܡܬܝ ܕܡܚܣܕܝܢ ܠܟܘܢ ܘܪܕܦܝܢ ܠܟܘܢ: ܘܐܡܪܝܢ
ܥܠܝܟܘܢ ܟܠ ܡܠܐ ܒܝܫܐ ܡܛܠܬܝ ܒܕܓܠܘܬܐ܂

(KJV version: *Blessed are ye, when men shall revile you, and persecute you, and shall
say all manner of evil against you falsely, for my sake.*)

Blessings when you are conspired against, scandaled and
accused falsely of corruption for my sake . . .

Health when your strength is sucked out, when you are
disunited and falsely classified as a waste of time, for my
sake . . .

Renewal when you are reproached and driven away by the
clamor of evil on all sides, for my sake . . .

When you are covered with insults like a sticky web, pulled
apart at the seams and wrongly labeled immature, for my
sake . . .

When you feel contaminated, dislocated, and feel an inner
shame for no good reason, it is for my sake . . .

Textual Notes

This Beatitude was translated as "Blessed are ye, when men shall revile you, and persecute you, and shall speak all manner of evil against you falsely, for my sake." This saying continues the thought of the preceding one and makes a transition to the surprising conclusion of the Beatitudes that follows.

Damhasdeen may mean reviled, reproached, derided, pitied, insulted, conspired against, or have one's strength sucked out. In its meaning of "contamination" the word carries the image of being covered with a sticky glaze of blame. *Radpin* is another form of the word used in the preceding Beatitude for "persecution" or "dislocation." *Mrin* refers to clamor, exaggerated noise, and any expression that would classify one falsely as *bisha* (see the Aramaic Lord's Prayer): unripe, evil, corrupt, immature, a diversion.

These unpleasant yet realistic occurrences are again expanded to a cosmic context by Jesus' conclusion.

Jesus said:

Haydeyn khadaw wa rwazw dagarkhun sgee bashmaya hakana geyr r'dapw l'nabiya d'men q'damaykun.

ܚܲܕܘ ܣܓܹܐ ܘܕܘܨܘ ܂ ܕܒܲܫܡܲܝܵܐ ܗܵܝܒ ܬܲܥܓܘܼܬ ܂

ܚܲܓܢܘ ܠܡܸܕ ܕܘܨܘ ܠܲܢܒܝܵܐ ܕܡܸܢ ܩܕܡܲܝܟܘ ܂

(KJV version: *Rejoice, and be exceedingly glad: for great is your reward in heaven: for so persecuted they the prophets which were before you.*)

Then, feel at the peak of everything and be extremely moved, for your natural abundance, already in the cosmos, has multiplied all around you (from the blows on your heart):

Do everything extreme, including letting your ego disappear, for this is the secret of claiming your expanded home in the universe.

Drink a drop—or drench yourself. No matter where you turn you will find the Name inscribed in light: it's all the One Creation.

For so they shamed those before you:

All who are enraptured, saying inspired things—who produce on the outside what the spirit has given them within.

It is the sign of the prophecy to be persecuted by circumstances.

It is the sign of the prophets and prophetesses to feel the disunity around them intensely.

These last lines were translated: "Rejoice, and be exceedingly glad: for great is your reward in heaven: for so persecuted they the prophets which were before you." The Aramaic version discloses that the first part of this translation is superficial. Jesus is not simply promoting "positive thinking" in the face of the injustices of society.

The root of the word *khadaw* refers to "everything extreme, the point or summit of something, gaiety or liveliness." It also presents the image of a drop of wine. The roots of the following word, *rwazw,* convey images of an inner movement of becoming extremely thin, of drinking or drenching, of a ray of anything, or of the breath. According to D'Olivet the root *rz* connotes an inner process of allowing the ego to become "thin," a secret of the desert mystics. The images of the breath and of drenching indicate other parts of this process. The combination says: when outer dislocation and persecution occur, use them to expand the territory within, allowing the *naphsha* (or subconscious self) to receive the attention it deserves and to become gradually clearer in relation to the divine purpose.

Awareness of the breath (in the fashion of the body prayers mentioned) can help one make this inner connection. Then one approaches life wholeheartedly: one can do things "to the extreme" and not apologize for being part of the prophetic and mystical heritage that Jesus renewed. The image of wine, associated with ecstatic states of consciousness, plays an imortant role in the mystical schools. As we saw in the Lord's Prayer, Jesus may also have been pointing toward the releasing power of the blood in a reference to wine: as I release who I thought I was, my outlook changes, and I can see more clearly the abundance of the universe.

The roots of *dagarkhun,* translated as "your reward," refer to this expanding sense of natural abundance, an organic movement reaching out at full length from the Source, yet fixed and grounded in material existence. It is another picture pointing toward the presence of God in all things. The verb *sgee* may be translated as "increased" or "augmented," but it too carries the image of an expansion from the center of abundance. This may indicate not only the cosmic center, but the expansion of the internal sense and center of abundance. As American poet Edna St.

Vincent Millay said in "Renascence": "The world stands out on either side no wider than the heart is wide." The blows on the heart can be felt as not only personally painful (which Jesus acknowledges) but also as an aid to opening a wider perspective of feeling and empathy with all creation.

In the final clause, the word *nabiya*, translated as "prophets," derives from a root that indicates divine inspiration or speaking by inspiration, also an ecstasy or rapture that germinates or bears fruit in the world. This word for prophecy, used throughout the Scriptures, means acting with the spirit that fills one. Jesus acknowledges that this is bound to be challenging and disturbing to society, because we cannot ignore the poor and outcast in our midst. Nor does he minimize the difficulties involved for those on the path of prophecy, as the translation "rejoice, and be exceedingly glad" might make it appear. In the Aramaic, the end of the Beatitudes strikes a bittersweet, but deeper note than that rendered from the Greek. It acknowledges that a certain amount of discouragement is natural and can be a reminder to turn within and renew before proceeding in the co-creation of heaven on and in earth.

The Beatitudes (One Possible New Translation from the Aramaic)

Tuned to the Source are those who live by breathing Unity; their "I can!" is included in God's.

Blessed are those in emotional turmoil; they shall be united inside by love.

Healthy are those who have softened what is rigid within; they shall receive physical vigor and strength from the universe.

Blessed are those who hunger and thirst for physical justice; they shall be surrounded by what is needed to sustain their bodies.

Blessed are those who, from their inner wombs, birth mercy; they shall feel its warm arms embrace them.

Aligned with the One are those whose lives radiate from a core of love; they shall see God everywhere.

Blessed are those who plant peace each season; they shall be named the children of God.

Blessings to those who are dislocated for the cause of justice; their new home is the province of the universe.

Renewal when you are reproached and driven away by the clamor of evil on all sides, for my sake . . .

Then, do everything extreme, including letting your ego disappear, for this is the secret of claiming your expanded home in the universe.

For so they shamed those before you:

All who are enraptured, saying inspired things—who produce on the outside what the spirit has given them within.

—OTHER SAYINGS—

Saying One

"Then one of them, which was a lawyer, asked him a question, tempting him, and saying, Master, which is the greatest commandment in the Law? Jesus said unto him, Thou shalt love the Lord thy God with all thy heart, and with all thy soul, and with all thy mind. This is the first and great commandment. And the second is like unto it, Thou shalt love thy neighbor as thyself."

(Matthew 22:35–39, King James Version)

Jesus said:

Detrahm l'marya Alahak
men kuleh lebak
wa men kuleh naphshak
wa men kuleh haylak
wa men kuleh rewhyanak. . . .
Detrahm laqriybak ayk naphshak.

ܕܬܪܚܡ ܠܡܪܝܐ

ܐܠܗܟ ܡܢ ܟܠܗ ܠܒܟ: ܘܡܢ ܟܠܗ ܢܦܫܟ: ܘܡܢ ܟܠܗ ܚܝܠܟ: ܘܡܢ ܟܠܗ ܪܘܚܢܟ

ܕܬܪܚܡ ܠܩܪܝܒܟ ܐܝܟ ܢܦܫܟ.

Jesus said:

From the deepest part of yourself, let love be born for the
rays of the One that shine around you . . .

Let this come from your whole heart—
the center of your life: your passion, courage, and audacity—
and touch your whole subconscious self—
that instinctive soul within which scatters and gathers.

From this self liberate your whole animal energy and
life force to flood your entire grasping mind with love.

This is the most important command [*raba*]—the first creative
movement that empowers all others. The second is like it:

Draw a breath of compassion for the one mysteriously drawn
to live near you: love that friend as you love the self that
dwells within—the subconscious that sometimes feels
separate and intruding.

Textual Notes

The word *Marya*, most often used with *Alaha* and translated "lord," stems from the root *mar*—the elementary rising principle that shines, lightens, and heats all things. If we open our eyes, we see all around us the light of the One shining through material creation. We are not asked to love God apart from the world but to see the One in all.

The word for "heart," *lebak*, comes from a root that means all passion, courage, audacity, and vitality, literally the heart or center of one's life. In the old roots the picture is given of an interior action of creative generation that expands from the center. (See also the discussion under the sixth Beatitude.)

From the heart, said Jesus, expand to include the whole *naphshak*. The Aramaic word *naphsha* is a key concept and may be found in the Hebrew *nephesh* as well as the Arabic *nafs*. It is sometimes rendered "soul" and sometimes "self" in the various translations of Jesus' words from the Greek. This has led to much unnecessary confusion, which is clarified in the Aramaic.

Naphsha could be called the "subconscious" or "instinctive" self. In the psychology inherent in native Middle Eastern mysticism, this self was seen as that small "I" or ego, which had its potential fulfillment in cooperation with God—the "I am that I am." The *naphsha* may be differentiated in various ways. Some parts of it may feel like "neighbors"—those who have been drawn to move near but are not part of one's family. Other parts may be cooperative with the divine light (*shem*) and guidance (*malkutha*). The whole project of existence was to unite the various parts of the *naphsha* in willing cooperation with the Source—*Abwoon*.

By loving the self, rather than rejecting it, one liberates all of one's instinctual life energy, the *hayla*. (See also the discussion under the last line of the Lord's Prayer.) This energy then rises, flooding the entire mind. In this case, Jesus uses the word *rewhyanak*, the roots of which refer to the lower mind: that which grasps, accumulates, and suffers the pains and anxieties of material existence.

In his statement about the "greatest commandment" (from the root *rab*—the movement that creates everything that follows), Jesus chose an expression embracing all elements of the Middle Eastern mystical law of manifestation. As one unconditionally loved the

Oneness, within and without, one would generate love from the heart and bring into God's light more and more of the *naphsha*. As this happened, the energy liberated would clarify one's feeling and direction in life. From this clearer intention would follow clearer thoughts and consequently clearer actions. In this way, loving God *enough* does everything.

In case his audience missed the point about the *naphsha* or self also being reflected outside, Jesus added the second part. The word usually translated as "neighbor" literally refers to those who have, somewhat mysteriously, been drawn to live near one. The roots of the word *laqriybak* reveal a principle that in Middle Eastern mysticism can only be called the tendency of parts to come together, of plants, animals, humans, and all beings to form a common bond or at least to clump together. Sometimes people consciously choose to live near one another, from a movement of sympathy. At other times the movement together is more mysterious and one cannot discern why one has the neighbors one does.

This is just like the cooperation of the *naphsha*, says Jesus. As one unites the "dwellers" within, one also becomes more responsible about and for those who dwell around one on the outside. Put another way, there is no proof of the inner spiritual work without corresponding action in community. As Jesus says elsewhere (Matt. 12:33), by its fruit you will know the tree—either edible or unripe.

More light is shed on this by the inner work of the Sufis, a mystical school arising out of the various desert ascetic groups both preceding and following Jesus. According to the traditional teachers of some Sufi orders, Sufism predates all the established religions in the Middle East and has survived through secrecy and a certain amount of "shape-shifting." In Sufism, an elaborate science of the *nafs* outlines various stages of evolution in the subconscious self—from animal to barely human to fully human to divine.

These stages seem to correspond to the degree of flexibility in the body, emotions, and personality to the will of God. As God's light enters the so-called darkness, the self loves it more and finds spiritual joy in everyday life. Ultimately, the division between self and God disappears: the self is found to be nothing other than the soul, a ray of the divine light that is never born and never dies. It is at this point that the mystic might say, with Meister Eckhart: "I see now that the eyes through which I see God are the eyes through which God sees me."

Saying Two

Jesus said,

   "Love your enemies."

   (Luke 6:27, 35, King James Version)

Jesus said,

Ahebw labwheldbabaykhun.

ܐܸܣܒܘ ܠܲܒܘܗܸܠܕܒܵܒܲܝܟ݂ܘܢ܀

Jesus said:

From a hidden place,
unite with your enemies from the inside,
fill the inner void that makes them swell outwardly and fall
out of rhythm: instead of progressing, step by step,
they stop and start harshly,
out of time with you.

Bring yourself back into rhythm within.
Find the movement that mates with theirs—
like two lovers creating life from dust.
Do this work in secret, so they don't know.
This kind of love creates, it doesn't emote.

Textual Notes

The word *ahebw* (root *hab*), used here for "love," differs greatly from *rahm*, used in the previous passage. Here one does not find the breath of compassion and mercy, but an even more mysterious, impersonal force, one that acts in secret to bring separate beings together to create new life. The root can also refer to planting seed, to a sexual relationship, and to the germ of a grain. This root has been used throughout native Middle Eastern mysticism and survives in a famous Sufi saying, *Mahabud lillah*, "God is the receiver and giver of love, as well as the love itself."

The word for "enemy," *bwheldbabaykhun*, conveys the image of a being out of time, moving with jerky, harsh movements. This is the Aramaic picture of "injustice." (Compare the discussion of "evil," *bisha*, under the seventh line of the Lord's Prayer.) The roots also present the image of one whose own inner void, inanity, and vacuity have caused that person to swell on the outside, like a boil. These conditions of the "enemy" are relative to the subject. That is, our personal enemy is out of step, impeding, vacuous, and puffed up in relationship to us. An enemy of a nation or the planet has those qualities in relation to a much wider sphere.

In this simple statement, Jesus presents the mystical law of relationships. To get along with other people, find the rhythm that harmonizes with their own and then bring them into harmony. Find within yourself that which fills their inner void and address that in them. The statement does not say anything about being "nice" to an enemy or letting that one walk over you.

Saying Three

Jesus said,

> "Whatsoever ye shall ask the Father in my name, he will give it you. Hitherto have ye asked nothing in my name: ask and ye shall receive, that your joy may be full."

(John 16:23–24, King James Version)

Isho said,

D'kul merem detheshaloon l'aby b'shemy
netel l'kun. . . .

Shalam watesbwoon
detehwey had wath'khon m'shamlaya.

ܕܟܠ ܡܕܡ ܕܬܫܐܠܘܢ ܠܐܒܝ ܒܫܡܝ ܀ ܢܬܠ ܠܟܘܢ܂

ܫܠܡ ܘܬܣܒܘܢ ܕܬܗܘܐ ܚܕܘܬܟܘܢ ܡܫܡܠܝܐ ܀܂

Jesus said:

All things that you ask straightly, directly, that you desire —
like an arrow to its mark,
like birds to their watering place —

from the Breathing Life of All, Father-Mother of the Cosmos,

with my *shem* —
my experience,
my Light and Sound,
my Atmosphere, my Word:
from inside my Name —

you will be given.

So far you haven't done this.

So ask without hidden motive and
be surrounded by your answer —
be enveloped by what you desire —
that your gladness be full —
that the joy of goals met here
    may continue its story to perfection in Unity —
that the animal life in you
find its lover in the Cosmos.

Textual Notes

The word for "ask," *detheshaloon*, summons forth a picture of traveling in a straight line, asking or desiring directly. The old roots present the image of a flock of birds coming to a watering place—they come directly, without hidden motives.

The word *b'shemy* is based on the same *shem* that occurs in the first line of the Lord's Prayer. That this phrase has been exclusively translated "in my name" without its other meanings is another tragedy of limited translation. It has led to the shell of Jesus' teaching being honored instead of the kernel. The word translated as "receive," *tesbwoon*, is based on the same root as that used in the fourth Beatitude: to be satisfied, enveloped, surrounded, or embraced by what one longed for.

Just as in the closing of the Beatitudes, the word translated as "joy" (*had*) may also mean a peak feeling, the experience of having a goal met, a desire fulfilled. Let this peak of feeling continue its movement to the end, says Jesus, using the word *m'shamlaya*. The root presents the image of a story continuing to its natural conclusion. Just as in moments of pain (considered at the end of the Beatitudes), says Jesus, let your peak experiences—the feeling of being fully enlivened—find their complement in the larger Life of the universe.

Resources for Further Study

Aprem, Rev. Dr. Mar. *Teach Yourself Aramaic*. Kerala, India: Mar Narsai Press, 1981.

Black, Matthew. *An Aramaic Approach to the Gospels and Acts*. Oxford: Oxford University Press, 1967.

D'Olivet, Fabre. (English version by Nayan Louise Redfield.) *The Hebraic Tongue Restored*. New York & London: Putnam, 1921. Original publication in French, 1815.

Eisler, Riane. *The Chalice and the Blade*. San Francisco: Harper & Row, 1987.

Errico, Rocco A. *The Ancient Aramaic Prayer of Jesus*. Los Angeles: Science of Mind, 1978.

―――. *Let There Be Light: The Seven Keys*. Marina del Rey, CA: Devorss & Co., 1985.

Errico, Rocco A., and Bazzi, Michael J. *Classical Aramaic, Assyrian-Chaldean Dialect, Elementary Book I*. Irvine, CA: Noohra Foundation, 1989.

Gwilliam, G. H. *Peshitta Version of the Gospels*. Oxford: Clarendon, 1901.

Jeremias, Joachim. *The Lord's Prayer*. Philadelphia: Fortress, 1964.

Lamsa, George M. *My Neighbor Jesus*. St. Petersburg, FL: American Bible Society, 1932.

―――. *The Holy Bible from Ancient Eastern Manuscripts*. Philadelphia: Holman, 1935.

―――. *Gospel Light*. Philadelphia: Holman, 1936.

―――. *New Testament Origin*. San Antonio: Aramaic Bible Center, 1976.

Robinson, Theodore H. *Paradigms and Exercises in Syriac Grammar*. Oxford: Clarendon, 1962.

Whish, Rev. Henry F. *Clavis Syriaca: A Key to the Ancient Syriac Version Called "Peshitta," of the Four Holy Gospels*. London: George Bell & Sons, 1883.

Resources for learning the grammar of the Aramaic language and other works by Dr. Rocco Errico may be obtained from the Noohra Foundation, 18022 Cowan Street, Suite 100-B, Irvine, CA 92714.

A cassette tape enabling one to learn to pronounce the Aramaic Lord's Prayer and Beatitudes, along with musical settings suitable for chanting and meditation, and prepared by Dr. Neil Douglas-Klotz, may be obtained from: Abwoon Study Circle, PO Box 361655, Milpitas, CA 95036 USA. Email: 73523.3177@compuserve.com Internet: http://www.wpo.net/desertflowers. In Europe, please contact: Dances of Universal Peace Tapes, 45 The Roman Way, Glastonbury, Somerset BA6 8AB England. Email: 100273.117@compuserve.com